NOT ALL SAINTS

by

Sean Thomas Dougherty

BITTER OLEANDER
P R E S S

2020

The Bitter Oleander Press
4983 Tall Oaks Drive
Fayetteville, NY. 13066-9776

www.bitteroleander.com
info@bitteroleander.com

ISBN #: 978-0-9993279-7-5

Library of Congress Control Number: 2020930136

Cover Design: Roderick Martinez

Back cover photograph of Sean Thomas Dougherty by Andy Denial

Cover illustration by Jane Ciminera

Printed by McNaughton & Gunn, Inc.
Saline, MI. 48176-0010
www.bookprinters.com

Distributed in the United States
by Small Press Distribution
Berkeley, CA. 94710-1409
www.spdbooks.org

Manufactured in the United States of America

ACKNOWLEDGMENTS

Thank you to the following journals which first published many of these poems, some under different titles and versions:

9 Mile: "ER"

The Bitter Oleander: "Poem Written in the Margin of Cloud Atlas," "Under Lilacs," "t"

Borderlands: "A Birch Tree In Winter," "Western Psychiatric Institute"

GTK Journal: "Cleveland Heights Monologue"

Here: "The Way Light Falls," "Sepia Postcard Near Atlantic City Circa 1987," "Those Notes We Compose," "Sonnet with a Sadness like Birds"

January Review: "Portrait of Townes Van Zant as a Murder"

KYSO Flash: "The Black Flags of our Bodies"

Louisiana Literature: "A Drawer A Window A Vault"

North American Review: "What Long Ellipsis"

Presence: "Poem with a Line from Kundera"

The Progressive: "Ask the Ghost Roads"

Salamander: "Some of the Hidden Things No One Wants to Talk about While Saying Goodbye"

Slipstream: "The Singing Wreck of Us"

Spillway: "If I Had Not Been Stillborn"

Sugar House Review: "The Men and the Quiet"

Talking River Review: "Against the Indifference of Angels"

Waxwing: "Praise Is to Claim a Departure from This World," "What Little Hobbies for the Dead"

Whiskey Island Review: "The Sound We Make When Falling"

World Literature Today: "Ask the Evening Light its Shape"

Some of these poems were published in the limited-edition chapbook *The Starlight Motel*, as part of the Punk Chapbook series by Epic Rites Press, Edmonton, Canada 2017.

Some of these poems appeared in the limited-edition collaborative chapbook with Lisa M. Dougherty, *The Answer is Not Here*, published by Night Ballet Press 2019.

"The Indifferent Wind Tells Me Any Dirt" appeared in the anthology *Like Light: 25 Years of Poetry & Prose by Bright Hills Poets & Writers*, published by Bright Hill Press 2017.

The title of "Poem Written in the Margins of Cloud Atlas" refers to the novel *Cloud Atlas* by David Mitchell. This poem began by collecting notations written in the margins of the novel.

"Poem with a Line from Kundera" borrows "the unbearable lightness of being" from the novel of that name by Milan Kundera.

CONTENTS

"In order to be a true revolutionary, you must understand love."

—Sonia Sanchez

"Half of my life I've been watching
Half of my life I've been waking up."

—The Walkmen

"You fools who ask what god is
should ask what life is instead."

—Ko Un, translation Suki Kwock Kim

for Lisa

NOT ALL SAINTS

LET ME TELL YOU A STORY

is another way to ask you to let me tell you
how to love me, to say why at night I curl

into the shape of a question mark: the summer Bobbie Womack
sang from the kitchen radio, the summer Gary

drowned in the quarry, and how I cut class
and walked everywhere that year, how I read Beckett

in the park I was seventeen I was a boy
whose chest was like a black balloon

someone was letting the air out of slowly.

THE WAY LIGHT FALLS

Between the two meter
maids, eating sandwiches
outside the House of Corrections.

The shadows of clouds
grow out of the sky.
Steam

rises from grates;
teenagers nod
under billboards.

Pawnshopped trumpets.
Iron locked gates,
the little lights

of barges
pass under the steel bridge
where every summer

someone fishing
finds a body.
Or the funeral

parlor,
the mortician's makeup
that made us look

as if we were in a musical
of *The Walking Dead*;
as if we leapt

off a rooftop
after we calculated
our last payment,

trying to decipher
what we witnessed
between the air's panes

is like the Desire
that webs us all,
or the way that light

falls

isn't failure.

SEPIA POSTCARD NEAR ATLANTIC CITY CIRCA 1987

In this winter light
like a wake
  I smoked
  beside a white girl
  as the bus departed

as the strangers left
  the station
one by one
  once more
I found myself
  watching the rain
  behind stained
windows (yellowed
  from smoke)

like a face
  in the distance

obscured
  a choir of them

  called

  like childhood

  in that abandoned farmhouse

  or the time
  I witnessed

across the railroad tracks
littered with needles
  the miraculous

  goats

stepping
with their long icicle beards

like the three wise men

heading toward the station

    of the cross

this girl carried the weight

    of what the rain cannot wash away

we watched the storm
drown the dark
what was there to say
if I had been left there
without spectators

before the pimps arrived
    the pimps who always arrive
towards the boardwalk
(there in the ugliness at the edges)

the rain let up
    I watched her walk
    down the block
    with her tiny suitcase

towards the vanishing point
of another life
I did not know
    more than her face
    and her jean jacket
    that spelled
(does it matter
    does it ever matter)
on the light
wind

you could smell the sea roses
           dying

AGAINST THE INDIFFERENCE OF ANGELS

I brought you a vomit bag,
and they took you away for your tests
behind the walls; I imagined the endless locked
drawers of narcotics. The methadone
nurse with the cane.
It wasn't a big dog, his mother said.
Her hair was dyed platinum blonde,
standing beside this small dark boy with cuts
all over his face and arms.
His mother was the largest woman
I had ever seen on this earth.
The intake nurse looked utterly unperturbed.
He didn't cry his mother said to the nurse.
Then turned to all of us and no one and said,
Look at him. All bit up and scratched.
Not one tear after the attack,
didn't cry until the police arrived
and shot that crazy mutt in the head,
and the wailing. Like life sawed
his little heart right in half.
Then the nurse took them behind the closed door.
I slept while they worked on you,
woke to find the boy returned to the waiting area,
both his arms bandaged to the elbow.
His mother walked beside him,
a miracle against gravity.
I don't mean to sound mean.
What I am trying to say is she
was utterly magnificent.
Her skin-tight leopard pants growled.
There was neither grief nor consolation
as they walked through the ER doors
and disappeared forever into their parallel life.
And I recalled a mural
I once saw in Chicago of migrant women
working in dusk light painted
on the side of a tenement.
A playhouse neon sign in winter.

The shine of eggplants
in the window of a Bronx bodega.
The red sky above the gravel freighters
on the great lake; old Cambodian men
fishing on the pier. I remembered
a pick-up truck, hauling pumpkins
on a county road in Ohio
and the white boys riding on the bed
giving everyone the finger:
these passing eavesdrops
of strangers and things
that should be little more than minutes
except they've come to mean
everything impossibly that is love.

NOT ALL SAINTS

The sky's blue paint
like the Sistine chapel

peeling. Tiny blue cherubs
fall into your mouth.

It's like we time warped to 1973, everyone's lapels
are wide. This dude at the counter

talks just like De Niro
in *Taxi-driver*,
the way my uncle did

after he returned from Nam;
I keep looking for you:
outside Porn shops

searching for a fix;
along the boardwalk,
in doorways where sequined

girls call out, *Hey Joe*
below huge billboards
for exuberant ruses;

in Busha's broth
cooking on the 14th floor.
I am nodding

on the fire-escape
of Desire,
soaked in bourbon.

~

In Motel yellow pages
I liked to add the names of Operas
to the listings for Drug Stores:

Don Giovanni's Dispensary;
Madame Butterfly Apothecary;
& my favorite Pharmacopeia Pagliacci.

~

There was a long wailing
I could not get out of my chest
no matter how much

I kept breathing.

~

It has been a long time
since I pressed my hand

into the bare bulb:

~

Wolves plunged through the snow,
& the great owl opened his eyes

like a decapitated head.

~

The white smoke of the refinery
plumed above the Eastside pier

like curse words in calligraphy.

~

At the corner bodega,
in the blue light of the television,

long after midnight,
this small woman

in a black hoodie, carefully
counted out dozens of dimes

from a tiny yellow plastic purse.

~

Some catastrophe swept away whole cities.
Fires burned across the plains,
& I was waiting in line, pissy & impatient

slightly drunk, I swore
for fucks sake—

(How often we do not see

until we are ashamed);
as she turned to leave,

I saw her face was a bouquet

of bruises.

A DRAWER A WINDOW A VAULT

The body is full of a far-away music.
Always the winds are folded

in the closed drawer

of the body on the subway
bench, the girl nodding

with a window

in her chest.
The train car of pews,

full of praying. This body
part of a simple story.
the magnificent disorder

~

of a green winter coat,
the tiny old woman beside me.
Her scarved head.
the rosary beads
in her pocket.

The crows in her eyes
and the roan horses
running in her hum.

(In this life who
have I loved?)

~

Under someone's sleeping lids.
This body, all of it
singing.

~

There is a drawer full of silence.
The silence of a sheet
of paper. Of a window

closed, or a vault. Or that word
I could not at first find: mausoleum.
The silence of heads bent

in prayer. The silent mourners
walking.
There is never really silence.

Always there are the hands
of the wind
trying to braid

the fallen leaves.
Always there is our breath
folded into our chests.

~

The people are rocking
back and forth.
I see sparks on the rail outside of the window.

If we were to crash, this train would be "a tomb."
but it is more like a drawer
full of secrets. Each secret

a stranger, a window, a vault;
a horse stumbles
breaks its leg.

(Who in this life
have I loved
besides myself?)

Look: the old woman
has fallen asleep
holding onto my hand.

THE MEN AND THE QUIET

In memory of his mother, his shirt started crying:
it detached from him right there in the vanishing light
and rose up like a great moth.
It was a lost cause, like a revolution.
Years ago, in the underground
tornado shelter his father built,
his father who worked in the steel mill
in Lorain—he was beginning to hear him more:
"Son, inside this strange skin is a star
bright as the flame I stare into that melts
ore." His father held out his hand
as if holding a bloody heart.
His mother, a minuet. His mother
so pained and strange, caught in her own grief.
She would break plates one after another:
white sharp shards, she'd pick up slowly
after she grew sick. He could tell you all this
with a quietness. Like horses on the side of a hill.
And then his shirt started crying. So hard it was
drenched. And he took it off. Right there
outside on break, smoking, and threw it.
And it rose up on the wind like a white swan,
And kept rising. And after that he was ok.
He drank his coffee cold.
The men who knew his father died.
"What happens when you get older
is you get over it. You buy flowers
to set on the table. You say your prayers.
You learn to live alone
the way you learned to love
everything
not dead."

LONG BEFORE WE WERE RUPTURED

When we were fifteen
      •   we stole peaches from the bodega
      •   the juice ran down our chins
when we were hungry, opaque
ghosts, the kind of children
on the side of the road
or a back alley
near a row of city housing
      •   in pamphlets
when all we wanted was an orchard
behind our trailer
and a sharp knife
he hung himself
from a birch tree in winter
      •   when we speak of dying
      •   we are double parked
when we were young
when we were scared
we ran into the arms of the men

who loved our mothers

outside the funeral home
in the February light
our breath
      •   the color of moth wings

WESTERN PSYCHIATRIC INSTITUTE

And then there is the light
that seeps from inside a pill

a boy is nodding
into his spittle

in a florescent room
a nurse bends over a form

as the gloved technician
places the paddles

on a man's chest
and then the flash

    •   there is a kind of quiet
    •   that cannot be named

a quiet white as salt
bright as dread

    •   that hangs from a branch
    •   of a birch tree in winter

that passes from one
body to another

like grief
and is released—

ASPHYXIATION

Once you let me borrow
your sneakers for gym class.
You had dark ringlets of hair.
We did not know we loved you.
There is no mention of mean;
there is no word I can find
to make you fly
from the back of the class, you hardly spoke.
The bruise above your eye
like the rusty sky: you stared out
over the schoolyard
sketching birds in a spiral notebook.
You did not smell.
You wore jeans and patches,
though you never danced.
You sat not too far away
when you ate
you were not alone.
You were there at the edges
a piece of what I was.
You gave me your toast once.
After decades I recalled you as Bobby
or Daren, but no it was
Davey, it was Davey.
We smoked a joint
behind the corner store
with Victor.
You stole your father's car
when none of us could drive.
He broke your arm.
They took him away.
What kills us
creeps us from behind.
Your mother died of emphysema.
All the cruelest deaths
are named with beautiful words.

THOSE NOTES WE COMPOSE

Across the bottle's lip
as if the dead are lurking.

White lilacs on the table
under the picture of Christ.

From a doorway,
the grotesque & the damned;

A menthol cigarette glowed.
A summer of cypress,

the silver dollar moon
above the back alleys

of broke, listening
through a fire-escape;

& a steel door opened:
the third shift spilled

from the warehouse dock.
No one can tell you the cost

for the sins we've sawed
in half—for the toll

at the intersection of parable
& piss— fallen off a stolen rig

at a sharp turn long ago—
her face of the Black Madonna.

Her bandaged wrist,
outside of the Polish Falcons;

the dogwood blossomed,
the girl so high it hurt

to hear her ask, how much?
At the corner of 3rd & Parade.

But all she wanted was to sell
the plastic Dyngus Day beads

she wore. She was matted hair,
perfume facing intravenous ghosts.

She was thin as the drizzling rain.
She snapped a necklace from her neck.

The red beads scattered
across the AM asphalt

like some fast, rough music
even mercy could not stay.

PORTRAIT OF TOWNES VAN ZANT AS A MURDER

Of crows, black suited ministers
on the telephone wire,
his guitar strings,
cawing for the coroner

to come as he picked
slow as a dirt road
leading to a rooming house
where someone fingered

a bullet into a revolver,
to shoot his best friend
in bed with his lover,
he sang like the hollow

chamber rings—

SONNET WITH A SADNESS LIKE BIRDS

You don't know how to approach strangers
anymore, much less anyone.
is there nothing but the distance of bus stations
and laundromats? It might as well be miles
to the dryer where she reads, or he knits
a scarf for some boy he adores.
For this is the heart: uselessly tore-lorn,
Yes, *love love love love love*. We say it
like stamping one's foot, in a puddle
out in the rain, towards no one
waiting for a face
to show itself, when what you most want
and most fear will leave you with a sadness
like birds, in the distance—

ASK THE HOUSE SPARROW

Blown one spring down the chimney
you flew through the open flue,

frantically around the living room,
until my father caught you in a box.

We let you go, undamaged.
No one-winged limping thing;

at the minor league ballpark, he hops
along the outfield grass;

who notices him but me? No,
the outfielder, a highly touted recruit,

bends his knees and appears to sing.
Ask the sparrow where it flies

after the last pitch was thrown,
to its nest high in the warmth

of the outfield florescent lights
that gleam above the tenement streets.

Your song is barely a song,
more a cheep, an eee eee i.

There is no weeping for the sparrow.
Ask her how sorrow flies.

You are always there at the edge of things.
Shivering in winter on a line,

you turn my hands to bread.
I scatter the crumbs across the snow

& you multiply pushing out the other birds;
you nest in the eaves.

Monogamous, you mate for life.
You do not steal: you are no bowerbird or black kite.

But what is the shape of the sky in your eye?
You curl into a ball the size of my palm.

You are a feathered word.
My father's humility.

You are the workers of the world,
there at the edge of things,

scrabbling over crumbs.
O Sparrow, what does the wind

wisp as it lifts your wings?
Your voicelessness is my own tongue.

ASK THE GHOST ROADS

For the names of the lynched.
     For the names of the good old boys
who shoot up the sign on the spot
     Emmett Till was murdered.
About plowed over Indian graves,
     ask the ghost roads about chicken bones,
and spent bullet casings,
     about a girl who went out for a walk
and never came home,
     about her mother and a can of castor oil,
about pig farmers and homemade sausage,
     about empty dressing gowns
and bent hangers
     about swollen eyes and sawdust
and the grr of a chainsaw
     and the crows.
Ask the ghost roads about trailers
     about sumac
about the same question asked
     over and over until there is only leaf-shudder
and no wind.
     About dry dirt spilling from a hand.
About barn burnings and first blooms
     about abandon
about the absence of an hour.
     About a wife and a wrong word
and a double wide
     rusting like a coffin
in the deluge,
     carrying someone
over the flood-sheared slope
     into the gorge
without a name
     or someone to remember
another body found in the underbrush
     in the spring

and the curve
        named after a dead man
but never a dead woman:
        we'd have to name every stream Sandra
name every hollar
           Lucille.

THERE IS ONE BLUE RIVER

"No one knows where it is
We know little but it is known"

—Mak Dizdar

There is one blue river we must cross. I read that in translation. I wondered if it was the Blue Danube. Perhaps it was the Volga, or the Vardar we walked beside in Skopje, among the Roman ruins, where I taught, where we gave the gypsy boy what we had every day so he could buy his tiny sister the pastry and dance his little dance. The joy we felt when his mother returned that winter and we saw her tussle his hair and he was able to go back to doing what older brothers are due. Or the Mississippi in Saint Louis where John was nearly shot trying to score, the bullet casing rang against the dark, or was it the Ohio where old Tony lost his job when the mill closed, he left to no one knows where the river takes us, the same with Timmy and the Allegheny, or was it the Susquehanna, or the Merrimack, alongside the closed down red brick mills, where we drank, where me and my friends would sit beside talking about leaving. Until we did, until we disappeared from that life and into another *no one knows where it is. We know little but it is known.* Or did I misread those words that were written decades ago in another language, in a country that no longer exists, was it not a blue river but did it say, *There is one blue cross we must climb,* like the one that rose high on the mountain above that city from another life, or the one we own inside our chests. How we make the sign when we touch our foreheads and our hearts, *beyond foreboding beyond doubt,* when we kneel and pray, we bow our faces to the dirt of our dead and offer the sky the nape of our blue veined necks.

ASK THE BREATH OF THIS BLUE HOUR

Ask the breath of this blue hour
if once we were winter rain
erasing the weight of salt
as a dead woman on a record
sings "I'll be seeing you
in all the old familiar places"
in a room far away
in another country
where we lived long ago
under a snow-capped mountain
after a time of war
where the old men drank
to forget what they had done
and to quiet their dread
still sometimes you stiffen
like an arm for a syringe
there is a kind of silence
that means mourning
in Macedonia, a kind of quiet
clung to over plum brandy
that we were once in winter rain
and the doves softly cooed
and the sleeping head of a dog rested
at the feet of a gypsy boy
who spit into his baby sister's mouth
when she was thirsty

ASK THE RAIN WHAT IT KNOWS

About leaving, about trouble,
about a man and a woman?
The train pulls out of the station,
the rain knows the answer
as it blotches her white dress.
What ink is used to write your name
across an old man's letter?
He's been waiting so long in the rain,
on the Williamsburg bridge.
Where were you when I heard my name
through the half-yellow streetlight?
Outside the subway station
the year Jolie died,
and they scattered her ashes
beside Emma Goldman's grave
and I turned to find no one
but the rain darkening the platform.
What was it you were scattering
across Lake Michigan?
Spattering against the cracked pane
of some tenement
across from the El
weaving its way through the trestle
of voices?
You at the table reading
about the dying bees.
Where were you when we lit
a thousand lanterns above the dirt tracks
and the stock cars,
and the bald children
brought there for charity
reached up their thin arms
towards the embered dark?
What towers and tenements
collapsed?
What empty stairwells?
What schoolyard without rhymes?

And here you come tap tapping
at memory's strange city
bringing back what it was
we were asking
on the smudged platform.
Hands clapping across the sky.

ASK THE DEAD LEAVES

The old neighborhood is long gone
my body is vanishing
almost airborne
in the dying pines
across the tracks
behind the cement plant
where we lived
I'd like to learn how to forgive
and not regret
deliver us to the little lights
along the bay racing
from your father's voice
we were swings
on the playground
in the depths of summer
and the sunlight that splashes
dappling dead leaves
ask them
who ate the heart of all that beauty
and the clear soprano upward
will answer
from the chest's cavity clear
with all the old songs
sung at so many funerals
bright and burning as whiskey
before the passing.

THESE STREETS OF LAMENTS

Not whole, parts like a life
witnessed through smoke
from the burning pyres
we passed on the Serbian train
among the shifting ruins
of memory's synapses
there are always your hands
opening like the doors to a church
in another country
where we lived long ago
where we once were winter rain
spattering against the apartment glass
across from the open-air market
where we bought blood oranges
from Spain & I read you testimonies
right after our daughter was born
& we carried her through the slush
& the streets of dead dogs
when you were young
in the winter rain, erasing
what was—
holding our daughter
out of the wind you were
cedar limbs & suicide
as you sang to her
like a dead woman on a record
the dark scratches
the needle played through
beside the kiosk selling cigarettes,
"I'll be looking at the moon
but I'll be seeing you"
when you lifted your face—

POEM FOR MY WIFE YOUNGER

Your father the union steward, just starting to weld
your mother working the 2nd shift at the plastics plant
they had not even met
when I was born
in Bellevue
a few floors from the lunatics
decades later I almost envy

for to live this life is to cage
the hurt we carry
to give it shape
the scars in our skin
unseen as the rain falls
and you are asleep
and the roof's music
the snore of the dark,
in your slight breathing
saws me when you first saw me
you said you wanted me to never be
unseen
and then the years of wreckage
the empty bottles
and the booze
the fitful alterations of the rain
re-stitching the dark's fabric
wind bowing the dogwoods
and the pines
creaking in the storm
shaking the rusted steel shed
where we still keep your father's tools
sharp enough to cut the dark
the steady downpour
of the dead
there is nothing more to say
except when I was born
there was a vacancy
like an empty room
inside my chest

like the spaces between the rain
for years when I was falling
forward
I could feel you there
in the absence of the air.

ASK THE EVENING LIGHT ITS SHAPE

Before there is sausage and bread
and blood red wine
like the light
over the great lake
are you a ship
or a sequin
something so tiny
it could be glued
to a fingertip
at the nail shop
where the Vietnamese girls
tie strings in their hair
and gossip
about the cute black boys
tossing a frisbee
at the high school track
across the avenue
this evening
the light passes
like a prayer
like through stained glass
or like birds
heading toward the darkening trees
the shape of sleep
the shape of that last dinner
and your leg brace
after the accident
and your cousin's wheelchair
and your grandfather's death
there is nothing near happiness
that summer night
we speak, after the light
passes
through us
what shape remains
in the darkened grass
we lay
you put out your cigarette

the fireflies rise
and all I can see
is your jawbone
the line of your throat
how many friends
are dead
or in prison
which is really
what I meant to ask
of the light
where they have gone
so easily
as one day passes
into dark
there are the shapes
of those we loved
and those to come
fluttering towards
what it is
is what shapes us
is not the light
it is the absence
cupped in our hands
like a moth
too soft to be heard

PARABLE OF A MARRIAGE

Perhaps it was in that silence we had first noticed her absence, you said she had gone off to find the bulbs of wish-flowers like when you were a girl and ran away for hours across the goldenrodded fields, ignoring the calls of your mother to come home. Or she had climbed the chain-link fence to the empty factory where I played baseball as a boy and sat like a monarch, bending her wings in the late summer light. It shouldn't have been but it was, joy had been what we let loose to wander away from us, to leave us bit by bit, when we weren't looking, when we were working, when we were raising our daughters and sons, how the candles flickered with the slightest wind of its passing, bit by bit, as they stopped speaking to us, as they left, on those nights when our voices became shards we finally knew it was nowhere to be found. And still we did what we were taught, how we were raised. We waited for their calls, and then the weddings came. We went about our days. We went to work, we did our jobs. And still when we thought the other was not looking, we reached with fingers to grasp when we thought we had once held, to grasp the empty air. Some nights we drank bottle after bottle of mildly expensive wine and told each other stories, always of them: calendars marked with birthdays, songs we sang them to sleep, first bike rides, bruises, impossible hopes and broken teenage hearts we nursed. But they were far away, now raising children of their own. And then there were the nights so simple it was as if the stars came down to sit with us, not saying a word. For what crime is something's absence, to know it had once been is more than enough, we could not lie, we were the lucky ones, as autumn fell, the dark rain pressed wet leaves like children's hands against the drive. The house was silent as paper cut-outs. We felt her, in this braided life the way her absence was the only way to know her. We were still as lilies on the table, waiting to open, in the tangled twilight between us. Together, we had gone on. How could we not? But for the quiet sake of joy.

TELL ME AGAIN

Under the birch
tree's bare limbs,
where we kissed,
and she was everywhere
and everything I could ever
wish what the snow wants,
bandaging the earth.

THE LITTLE BIRD THAT RATTLED

her air conditioner was trying to stay cool/got sucked in,

and for a while its dying/was filling the rooms/she slept

in/how often this happens in ways we never hear /the clatter

never finds us/so we cannot at least/ hold the tiny feathered

/song in our palms/and grieve it gone/offer it a word/ or

two/ like a prayer/ wrap it in a paper towel/or bury it in the

backyard/ dirt we dig /and in this way/we honor what was

lost/ it is not this/ too often/the silent/ losings pass us/

unawares/perhaps we need to/when doing nothing/ like the

dishes/every now and then/for them/mutter/something—

WHAT LONG ELLIPSIS

It's not that I am lost but that I carry the ones I've lost inside me so much I forget exactly who I am the only world or such is sleep and fullness and hissing wilderness in alleys where raccoons rise to show their sharp teeth on East side streets where empty vials litter yards I stumble drunk from the Polish Falcons where I shot pool with a welder cranked out of his mind with an aloneness I don't even know was there the face of Matt with his late night binges and a window sill of pills he stole from the hospital where he lit people's bones with radiation, his imagined trephination, telling us "sometimes I can see another kind of light inside them" swallowed Percocet and valium and shared, or Roger with his cocaine and his crates of vinyl he carried spinning house parties and then the nose bleeds and the palpitations and the speed and the throwing things and the bad women and he was gone to a prison in somewhere Tennessee, his late night calls and rants. I bet you can name a dozen more. Is it guilt or grief we carry, married to the rain I walk in every downpour bearing shame. What city of amnesia do I search for? Delirium or laudanum. Oxycodone or valium lifted by stoned attendants from the old folks' homes that line the edge of the frozen lake. There is never silence to help me through the daily noise. The whispering of voices is a hallway in my head. I carry Ohio across my chest. Those older neighbor girls who beat me with a stick and took off my pants. They beat me and beat me with a stick and still I did not tell or beg. Day after day, week after week they honed me into a perfect blade. And then we moved, and I was saved. I was six years old. I can still inside my head hear cicadas' violent blaring as the last time I walked up those stairs. I had survived to claim this life, despite what long ellipsis.

THE SINGING WRECK OF US

What is passing passes like this: how in spring
when the melting begins, the ice breaks,

the groan & ache of it loud enough to fill the sky.
The sudden fractures unseen until the shatter.

Which is why I hold your swollen hand
& see the constellations of the wounds in your skin

& try not to make something more of them than pain,
but we both know there must be something more.

Something to lift our lives
& drop us down across town,

or in a hospital where they pronounce you cured.
But we both know this pain

will only end in a formal light.
To go this way is common

as the light that creeps over the lake
this humid summer morning, walking

quietly on tired dog feet. It is too early
for the children to be not asleep,

I hear their tiny feet running in search of the dog.
They pull his tail and chase him barking.

I am not trying to say anything I fear
except now it is the dog days of summer

where we eat & sweat, & inside my chest
is a church wall, somewhere to pray,

or am I refugee, asking for amnesty?
No, it is *the now* where we are refugees.

Starlight even each evening hurts my eyes.
If there is nothing beatific to claim from this life

all I can claim for us is this your razored breath
as I watch you fall to sleep on the couch,

or the way our daughters
play a game they've invented, they sit eyes closed,

face to face & touch each other's cheeks
with their fingers & do not say a sound,

as if they are speaking their own secret
dialect, almost purring, before one suddenly screams

& pushes the other down, & they tumble,
falling together, teaching themselves about pain,

& how it passes, how everything passes—

THE INDIFFERENT WIND TELLS ME ANY DIRT

If I die on the highway
you know what to do,
write me an elegy
to save the world, so my spirit
will hear it and joyously float
over tenements
where children are playing violins,
and the brick walls are painted
foundation to roof
with sunflowers
and portraits of Dizzy Gillespie.
Believe I would die for that.
Believe I would do anything to save
you who despite
every day in one way
or another, dies too
(what more can our words do)
and at shift's end
is reborn. We keep going on—

THE BLACK FLAGS OF OUR BODIES

Dear J,

I am writing this to you from the back porch. In the frantic drowse and dive
of the late summer bees. J, this world might give you invisible scars, but I heard
from your sister about your brother being moved across state, and how it seems
to be dragging you to the ditch of purple weeds. I am sorry he doesn't know
your name anymore, and the state closing his home and moving him a hundred
miles away. The skin grows all sorts of things. A green winged fly buzzes in
our ears. So arbitrarily hurtful, the state of such dispositions is the most difficult
to handle I find too, because what can we do? They ship who we love from one
hospital to the next, unheld in their own spittle.

And what do we do with the anger we carry? We punch our own bruises. And
even Emmy Lou Harris singing on a *Magnolia Wind* doesn't seem to help.

At least your brother Peter will be somewhere, rather than nowhere stumbling,
like so many without speech. That is something. Remember that that is some-
thing. How many of us are refugees with no port, no country we can name.
The insults they hurl at us. The damned and the poor are the damned. All we
have are the songs and psalms we carry inside us. There is no curfew for love.
Out in the fields. The black flags of our bodies

unfurl. We blow kisses to our children, smell the wind through their hair, and
you have to realize that this is life, that is all we get, that most of life is all this
suffering. The long stroll to become nothing. We pummel the bag, we punch
the wall. This really is it brother. This thin air. That doesn't stop and we just
keep going, doing what little we can for how few or many we can along the
way. That's all God asks of anyone. He doesn't ask for more. You and I are
stronger than any seraphim. So that's why he brings us all this shit, because
we're still here. Even on this dusky afternoon, when my woman is changing
her bandages again. To pray and love our sick and our old. So many don't have
nobody. Nobody to share such silence, so that's why I'm writing you this letter,
to send the scent of cut clover and the lilacs blooming and the dying elms and
the drowsy shush and fall of late summer bees.

UNDER LILACS

For you the wind rests inside my shirt pocket, presses its cheek
to my chest. The ground is covered with yellow and brown edged
leaves, the dog has been eating the lilac tree again, the ground
covered with chewed thorns. The air is cool damp and speaks
of dread, as every summer passes how many will we save?
A sparrow lifts her head. Our daughter sits on the crushed lid
of the plastic sandbox spinning twigs and this you made up of
the dead and the switchblade of your small shoulders
I press my hands into

the day is cool, and the night will bring the changing of the bandages,
long after
lullabies the world I dread full of your voice not a voice, chord less,
dissonant sound of pain, and then the silence of the body writhing
as you rock on sleepless shore until it subsides, ebbs its tide.

For you so hard   recall when the magnolias were in bud and the asphalt
 too hot to walk in bare soles. Those simple days to tell the story
of these years of losing, and yet we go on knowing there will be for you no
            rocking chair
to sit and watch the waves, and our daughters who will grow
so tall, and razored. How will they carry this loss, of you this you
who held them like a tune. For you our oldest how she stole your perfume,
a bottle
hidden in your drawer and sprayed herself to smell like you, this you
long after you are gone

I will keep only what I can carry. For what I hold onto is this holy day
the cold and blooming late September light, the dog chewing on the lilac
            thorns,
our daughter humming her little song, one without structure
or restraint, tumbling like a yellow leaf in the wind,
is it a dirge, or a hymn? As the dog, chewing on lilac thorns, pricks
his ears up suddenly at nothing—

t

our youngest daughter stands, arms
straight in the twilight, a stick

figure like a small
t, typeset against the dark

page of your dying—

THE SOUND WE MAKE WHEN FALLING

There's no time for traffic lights. The ghosts are everywhere. What is God but a return or a rerun, as the town next door burns on all the televisions. I want to tell you a word like cloud, or wind. Perhaps a whistle, through the black trees. But all I have to offer is this basket of plums, the one with a bruise—see the red spider there what is it waiting for? Imagine its web, glistening with dew. Or hiding in the leaves. Or the plums, if we kill it, they will taste so cold. One joy I want to remember, when we awaken to the rain rushing through the eaves. It is like this all the time: there is a woman I know whose adult son died in a car accident, he was rushing towards no place important, as we all are, so often scrimmaging anxious. The runes we cannot read. What I am trying to say is we no longer eat our afterbirth or name the stars. Cassiopeia. Gomeisa, the bleary eyed. I am so tired, surrounded by this infinite dark. Come home I say. To the house with the lights turned off. Can you see her? In his room, no tongue can explain her grief. Like a word written with both Roman & Greek letters. There is no sound for this. So I begin to draw what I cannot spell. For what is the cost, or the claim, or the cable I would send anyways when everywhere I go there are bodies being buried & burned, & such loss runs deep as the waters of Lethe, this terribly foreign & familiar helplessness, this unforgiving alphabet we must excavate & earn—

POEM WITH A LINE FROM KUNDERA

I would like to be loved the way a child loves
       a star.
Loved with a silence, the way smoke hovers
       like a person at rest.
I want to tell you what is stationary
       but in reverse, like the way the Big Bang
will eventually reverse
       is most revealing, a form
of furious folding
       backwards towards everything's birth,
like a body bearing its knees
       to its chest
in *the unbearable lightness*
       of being
born, or the weight of grief.
       Often, I suspect the heaviness
of objects
       is less than they look.
Like a human soul
       if you weighed it.
But sometimes you realize a person
       is in pieces—shattered or broken, we say
into amber-like-shards.
       Sweep them up and place them
on the scales
       of your palms.
And there they will shine,
       and there you will find
that love is
       the exact weight
of starlight—

CLEVELAND HEIGHTS MONOLOGUE

I was born under the roof of rain that makes love possible.
        I borrowed an
incomprehensible book from the old Jewish woman Mrs.
Moskowitz who lived in the flat
below. She was always giving me bread. She was always
        yelling at me in
Yiddish. There were always things to borrow like clothespins,
        things she was losing
like teeth. Her nephew pasted broadsides for radical meetings
        on the walls. She was the one
my mother paid to sew my sneakers when I ripped them.
        The Hum of the old
black Singer, her flat shoe on the pedal like a drummer. I ran
        young & naive
as April light, shapeless as water. Once though they were
dragging people into cruisers, I drank my glass of milk. It
        wasn't my fault I heard her friend say,
the word interrogation, the word detention. I watched her put
        eggshells in the coffee
grounds. My aunt told me she had a box with the ashes of her
still born child. I was
born into a narrow happiness. What I bore
        I begged like an unexpected burden. I gave my allowance
        to the street
musicians, the man with the violin and the hat. I was born
from a wound, the names
of small towns, the screech of tires, the labyrinth of days, all
        the long doldrums like
the parking attendant at the hospital who took my ticket. The
        long slimy trails of snails
on the stoop: the looping hand in a tasseled book the Rabbi
        read; I want to understand the shame of it, the shine of the
        black urn. A few
words in Yiddish. Her young relatives with the long faces
        came and sat on the low stools. The black sheets
over the windows, the bearded men.

Even the branches wept. The old women rocked
praying in Hebrew. Outside the sheeted window. There is so
        much to say etched
with words. Elegies in the troubled light. A loneliness I
        cannot answer. A grief
waist deep in amniotic fluid and ash. Only the early falling
        snow as
I sat at a diner counter; the waitress named Alma
        slid a Kennedy half
dollar across the counter. *Alma* I asked is that dawn? No,
        that is Alba, Alma is *soul*. In Spanish she said, I know so
        little. *Entiendo poquito*. Looked out at winter erasing the
        world, said, *it amazes me how fast we disappear*,
as easily as opening and closing a door. I sipped the dark
        from my coffee. The black wick
of my heart snuffed in my chest. Afterwards, I pulled my hat
        down over my eyes and walked through the snow towards
        the bus.
        In the far distance, the flames from the last steel plant
        lit the sky—

ER

I drank my paper cup of water
(more ash for my forehead)
& then I repented of any sin
on a knee right there by the water cooler
this language like learning
a new alphabet of reprieve
the old woman slumped into her snoring
the child who will not stop screaming
the nurses no longer wear hats
every day we have nowhere to go
so we ended up west
of the projects (I paid the cab fare)
I stopped weeping
to watch the janitor sweep
the fat cop bending over a form
I was fully aware of my skin
was little more than a bobbing bag
of blood
all of us so fragile & broken
even the boy pushing the vending machine
buttons & screaming
someone may have just died
we all wore winter coats
even the woman who they tore from the room
into a straight-jacket
she was bleeding from her chin
the woman speaking Spanish was inconsolable
the black daggers of her mascara
cut her face

~

They hit her with a needle in a different vein
(this was years ago)
you drew a sunflower on the back of every menu
when we huddled this went on for a long time

you pulled the tail of evening into dark
you said you've never been afraid

when you didn't know what to do
the building we lived in had no elevator
to carry us back to the metronome
of the broken faucet & the windows painted shut

all winter the tin whistle
of the radiator's hiss

at the first snow covering the lawn
you flopped down to flap your hands
when you stood up
I reached out
I am still reaching
for days after
there was only an outline
of where you were—

IF I HAD NOT BEEN STILLBORN

If I had not been stillborn. Amid the black chest of the factory I became a breath. In the lungs of the mine. Or I if not the solitary piano unplayed. Or I alone in the closet. Or I with the spools of fingers weaving orchestrations in the air. I am always empty. I am a breath, hollow or is it hallowed? If I had not been stillborn, I would have been a ball rising ruby red through the playground, a shout, a sentence, a hallelujah heard in a mother's ears, quietly as a lisp or a lullaby. Or would I have been a room entered and a shutter? Would I have been a closed door? Would I have been a window? If I had not been stillborn, I would have been a window. Gazing over the streets of my father, watching my mother close the door and leave for work. The weeping she makes with her steps, her bent back, the weight she carries, the weight I lift, I reach for her face on the bus. I pull the chord like the one that wrapped around my neck. There is a music even in death. I am the voice she hears without hearing. I am the space of her empty arms, and when she turns suddenly to look at nothing, I am the space in the air—

WHAT LITTLE HOBBIES FOR THE DEAD

I drink nothing less than the blues. I have no other habits left. Though sometimes at Wegman's bakery I stand there sweating, inhaling the breath of just baked bread. The only citizenship I claim is the mountain and the great lake. Perhaps the only pledge we need is *The Leaves of Grass*, or Thoreau's diction to always resist? What do we care if all that is left is ruins, it is where we have always lived. Once though when I was small, and my mother took me to the coast of Maine, I saw the wild sea roses rim the road and cliffs like a thorned crown. Or in the marketplace in Cleveland, the old Hungarian woman who handed me a great length of sweet sausage wrapped so quick yet carefully in white paper & then the day's newspaper taped together with masking tape. Is that our true flag? The untamed and the stained? Who are our people those who emerge with poor unturned faces from doorways and windows, then run shouting despite the evidence each day I am waiting for a sign, a spark, I test the direction the wind might turn, & what will come with it? All of us tumbling down the avenues & roads looking for something, & like birds who cursive across the sky, who are we if not something written with the body's ink across the page of the workday's dwindling hours, some testament to survival? Step by step, shift by shift, we pass even the saints. We become something closer to our dead. I ask for no wager except that others who come after to suffer a little less. In this life is another & another, & another that is this human nest. This daguerreotype divine or damaged— for what is damaged is closer to divine. I look up just in time to see a wafer of moon dissolve into the mouth of the dark.

PRAISE IS TO CLAIM A DEPARTURE FROM THIS WORLD

The gerund of my daughter, this June day in the backyard pool splashing she seems to forget the space between earth & sky. Afterwards we walk along the splintered plywood of the pool where wild strawberries grow; we bend to eat the berries, afterwards her face covered in tiny red commas. We've become exiles from the ordinariness of our lives. Our daughter with her wild nettled hair. If only my grandmother were still alive to teach her to speak with crows. Or the ancestors from the North of Ireland. The windswept cliffs of Donegal. Or my great great lost cousins who tailored, studied and lived by *Tzedakah* in the Carpathian *shtetls*. This blood in us that seethes like centuries of genocide & violins. This world of passports & police dogs, stun bombs & Coltrane. As my daughter now runs with her sister across the sun-dead grass, I cannot even wish the bastards pain, the ones with their yachts & ledgers, their skyrise plantations, their necrocide, the ones for whom the Drones drop missiles from the sky. We are not refugees in the green & orange light of dusk. We are punctuation marks against the silence. And we will rise. A line of crows gathers to watch us from a telephone line. This is an ache beyond form we carry in our skins. The way animals can tell when a storm is coming, or the way our cat can see the beings who live in shadows. But death is our domain. We daughter nothing less. We can kill over a shiny bauble. We can kill just to see something die. When I couldn't get rid of the red ants with water, I poured gasoline into the dirt & lit the match. My daughters danced like dervishes at the flames. As the dirt burned the tiny bodies into ash. We are the myths we carry. But the Gods are not beyond our bodies, blazing the night into a chorus of croaks. The frogs calling to each other from the drainage ditches along the railroad tracks. Tracks like a lattice of infinitives to climb. Around the planet the amphibians are dying & no one knows why. They are the first to go & then us. It is night now. We are no more than a biography of lilac leaves my youngest daughter ate. My daughters are having dreams of tambourines & pulling the wings off bees. My oldest one snores, like the dog. You see I am trying to tell you something, but no matter how I start it, I never quite get there. I return to what is around us. But joy keeps interrupting the familiar phonemes of grief digging my fingers into the earth.

SOME OF THE HIDDEN THINGS NO ONE WANTS TO TALK ABOUT WHILE SAYING GOODBYE

We were walking past your dead grandfather's house, and I left you as if through a door in the air. I wanted to tell you, but you were speaking in the streetlight's glow. Your words made a room where he was not dying but playing a board-game I did not know and there you were. You must have been five years old. It was November and there was snow on the windowsill. You wore a yellow jumpsuit. At this point I was faced with a decision. Another kind of door leading outward opened. I cannot tell you more, I could not see. This is the trouble with light: the little blooms of your eyes were filling everything.

POEM WRITTEN IN THE MARGINS OF CLOUD ATLAS

To seek the other in the one

to search for the other in the one

to follow the other in the one

to forget the other in the one

you are my blue glass guitar

the bandaged light of your hands

when you come you come as

the afternoon's tremulous wailing

you are

when you yell at the children

I used to think that is not you but that is you too

it is not that I trusted you, but I trusted what you could become

to arrive in language that reflects those states of being, so they defy words

our bodies are but signs for us to find one another

across time and space, I taste your breath as haling the scent of earth

after a hard rain

you are a hard rain falling

endlessly hillbilly in the month of love

they forgot peach trees and the pity of mountains

or what I've come to find is tame

like a wind through an orchard suddenly dies

and the bruised fruit on the ground

we lay inside all of that rotting

the humming of the bees

I am a fallen thing

you are the humming of the bees

you are the bruised

she doesn't want us to see the bandages on her foot, so she rarely leaves the house now without her plastic boot

I load the celluloid in the film

our lives are dark rooms like movie theaters that suddenly become scenes of flickering light

before I met you was the trailer

there is a grammar to remembrance, an alphabet to longing

you are the letters in the alphabet of longing I never learned to write

I am trying to tell you there is a chance now, even for people like us

what is the refrain of the rain

drenched in the downpour outside the train station

save our pity what I am after I cannot buy anyways

you are something that can never be bought

we sell ourselves so easily

we become slaves

wren-like your wrists you unwrap the bandages

to suddenly sing

at the back of the house and the kitchen is hot with black pot blues bubbling
up

I stared into the puppet theater window.   I saw the reflection of myself and
our oldest daughter. For a long moment I could not tell the difference between
myself and the wooden face of the old puppet man

the strings we attach to our shoulders

to touch your face was to open the body like the way a word (Waldrop
wrote) opens the body

to enter a kind of trance

I am a word

you are a word

clandestine

razor

typeface

a kind of calligraphy we read upon the clouds

to write a script that unravels as it begins

I watch you bandaging your feet, the wound that never heals. At night, you take the pills. Barbiturates to numb the ache. I watch you nod into your chest. The room is cool, so   I breathe as you rest. Some days I can do little more than breathe as you rest

Our daughters are a kind of typeface we have invented to speak a language that did not exist to speak what we could not even spell. Only when we watch them as they run, and we glance at one another can we tell each other without a word what we could not before they arrived

what we teach our daughters will destroy worlds

to burn the page

to write with the ashes of a burned page

I lay down into the empty bed at night, the bed made emptier by the simple fact of another pillow

she sleeps on the couch now with her wounded foot lifted to one side

when she looks at you the light is looming

she is the looming light

I am not thinking what is locked in form except to say the way that laughter leaves a body

you are what laughter I have left

even the moon is laughing

wearing her spooky garments

Halloween, we limped from door to door. The lilac branches were bare. You walked holding my arm like an old woman, decades before you were supposed to die. The street was full of howling children. Later, our daughters unwrapped their loot and left the wrappers on the living-room floor. After we put them groaning to bed, we laid on top of all that crinkling celluloid-like paper. We gently traced each other's faces. We were an alphabet of longing. You were traveling on an outbound train toward a distant station where I was waiting

I would have recognized you if you arrived as anyone.

ABOUT THE POET

Sean Thomas Dougherty was born in New York City and grew up in Brooklyn, Ohio, and New Hampshire. He is the author or editor of eighteen books including *Not All Saints*, winner of the 2019 Bitter Oleander Library of Poetry Award; *Alongside We Travel: Contemporary Poets on Autism* (NYQ Books 2019) and *All You Ask for is Longing: New and Selected Poems* (BOA Editions 2014). His book *The Second O of Sorrow* (BOA Editions 2018) received both the Paterson Poetry Prize, and the Housatonic Book Award from Western Connecticut State University. His awards include the Twin Cities College Association Poet in Residence, a US Fulbright Lectureship to the Balkans, two Pennsylvania Council for the Arts Fellowships in Poetry, and an appearance in *Best American Poetry*. He has worked in a newspaper plant, as an untenured college lecturer, and in a pool hall. He now works as a care giver and Med Tech for various disabled populations and lives with the poet Lisa M. Dougherty and their two daughters in Erie, Pennsylvania. More information on Sean can be found at seanthomasdoughertypoet.com

THE BITTER OLEANDER PRESS
Library of Poetry

TRANSLATION SERIES

Torn Apart by Joyce Mansour (France)	—translated by Serge Gavronsky	$14.00
Children of the Quadrilateral by Benjamin Péret (France)	—translated by Jane Barnard & Albert Frank Moritz	$14.00
Edible Amazonia by Nicomedes Suárez-Araúz (Bolivia)	—translated by Steven Ford Brown	$11.00
A Cage of Transparent Words by Alberto Blanco (Mexico)	—a bilingual edition with multiple translators	$20.00
Afterglow by Alberto Blanco (Mexico)	—translated by Jennifer Rathbun	$21.00
Of Flies and Monkeys by Jacques Dupin (France)	—translated by John Taylor	$24.00
1001 Winters by Kristiina Ehin (Estonia)	—translated by Ilmar Lehtpere	$21.00
Tobacco Dogs by Ana Minga (Ecuador)	—translated by Alexis Levitin	$18.00
Sheds by José-Flore Tappy * (Switzerland)	—translated by John Taylor	$21.00
Puppets in the Wind by Karl Krolow (Germany)	—translated by Stuart Friebert	$21.00
Movement Through the End by Philippe Rahmy (Switzerland)	—translated by Rosemary Lloyd	$18.00
Ripened Wheat: Selected Poems of Hai Zi ** (China)	—translated by Ye Chun	$21.00
Confetti-Ash: Selected Poems of Salvador Novo (Mexico)	—translated by Anthony Seidman & David Shook	$18.00
Territory of Dawn: Selected Poems of Eunice Odio (Costa Rica)	—translated by Keith Ekiss, Sonia P. Ticas & Mauricio Espinoza	$20.00
The Hunchbacks' Bus by Nora Iuga *** (Romania)	—translated by Adam J. Sorkin & Diana Manole	$18.00
To Each Unfolding Leaf: Selected Poems (1976-2015) by Pierre Voélin (Switzerland)	—translated by John Taylor	$25.00
Shatter the Bell in My Ear by Christine Lavant (Austria)	—translated by David Chorlton	$18.00
The Little Book of Passage by Franca Mancinelli (Italy)	—translated by John Taylor	$16.00
Forty-One Objects by Carsten René Nielsen (Denmark)	—translated by David Keplinger	$18.00
At an Hour's Sleep from Here (Poems 2007-2019) by Franca Mancinelli (Italy)	—translated by John Taylor	$28.00

* Finalist for National Translation Award from American Literary Translators Association (ALTA)—2015
** Finalist for Lucien Stryk Asian Translation Award from American Literary Translators Association (ALTA)—2016
*** Long-Listed for National Translation Award from American Literary Translators Association (ALTA)—2017

ORIGINAL POETRY SERIES

The Moon Rises in the Rattlesnake's Mouth by Silvia Scheibli	$ 6.00
On Carbon-Dating Hunger by Anthony Seidman	$14.00
Where Thirsts Intersect by Anthony Seidman	$16.00
Festival of Stone by Steve Barfield	$12.00
Infinite Days by Alan Britt	$16.00
Vermilion by Alan Britt	$16.00
Teaching Bones to Fly by Christine Boyka Kluge	$14.00
Stirring the Mirror by Christine Boyka Kluge	$16.00
Travel Over Water by Ye Chun	$14.00
Gold Carp Jack Fruit Mirrors by George Kalamaras	$18.00
Van Gogh in Poems by Carol Dine	$21.00
Giving Way by Shawn Fawson **	$16.00
If Night is Falling by John Taylor	$16.00
The First Decade: 1968-1978 by Duane Locke	$25.00
Empire in the Shade of a Grass Blade by Rob Cook	$18.00
* *Painting the Egret's Echo* by Patty Dickson Pieczka [2012]	$14.00
Parabola Dreams by Alan Britt & Silvia Scheibli	$16.00
Child Sings in the Womb by Patrick Lawler	$18.00
* *The Cave* by Tom Holmes [2013]	$12.00
Light from a Small Brown Bird by Rich Ives	$14.00
* *The Sky's Dustbin* by Katherine Sánchez Espano [2014]	$12.00
* *All the Beautiful Dead* by Christien Gholson [2015]	$12.00
* *Call Me When You Get to Rosie's* by Austin LaGrone [2016]	$12.00
Wondering the Alphabet by Roderick Martinez ***	$30.00
Kissing the Bee by Lara Gularte	$14.00
* *Night Farming in Bosnia* by Ray Keifetz [2017]	$12.00
Remembrance of Water / Twenty-Five Trees by John Taylor	$21.00
The Stella Poems by Duane Locke	$16.00
* *Ancient Maps & a Tarot Pack* by Serena Fusek [2018]	$15.00
**Not All Saints* by Sean Thomas Dougherty [2019]	$16.00

* Winner of The Bitter Oleander Press Library of Poetry Award (BOPLOPA)
** Utah Book Award Winner (2012)
*** Typography, Graphic Design & Poetry

All back issues and single copies of *The Bitter Oleander* are available for $10.00
For more information, contact us at info@bitteroleander.com
Visit us on Facebook or www.bitteroleander.com